REALLY RADICAL REPTILES & AMPHIBIANS

AMAZING ANIMALS

BELL'S
HORNED FROG
Ceratophrys ornata

Leslee Elliott

Sterling Publishing Co., Inc. New York

With Love to SCOTT,
Who Collects Creepy Crawlers

Library of Congress Cataloging-in-Publication Data

Elliott, Leslee.
    Really radical reptiles & amphibians/Leslee Elliott.
        p.   cm. — (Amazing animals)
    Includes index.
    ISBN 0-8069-1268-5
    1. Reptiles—Miscellanea—Juvenile literature.   2. Amphibians—
Miscellanea—Juvenile literature.   [1. Reptiles.   2. Amphibians.]
    I. Title.   II. Series: Elliott, Leslee.   Amazing animals.
    QL644.2.E44   1994
    597.6—dc20   94-26053
                                                                    CIP
                                                                    AC

Designed by Judy Morgan

Edited by Dr. Nancy B. Simmons, Assistant Curator, Department of Mammalogy, American
Museum of Natural History

Cover photo: Parson's Chameleon by Kevin Schafer and Martha Hill, TOM STACK AND ASSOCIATES

1 3 5 7 9 10 8 6 4 2
Published by Sterling Publishing Company, Inc.
387 Park Avenue South, New York, N.Y. 10016
© 1994 by Leslee Elliott
Distributed in Canada by Sterling Publishing
% Canadian Manda Group, One Atlantic Avenue, Suite 105
Toronto, Ontario, Canada M6K 3E7
Distributed in Great Britain and Europe by Cassell PLC
Villiers House, 41/47 Strand, London WC2N 5JE. England
Distributed in Australia by Capricorn Link (Australia) Pty Ltd.
P.O. Box 6651, Baulkham Hills, Business Centre, NSW 2153, Australia
Printed and bound in Hong Kong
All rights reserved

Sterling ISBN 0-8069-1268-5

CONTENTS

GREEN CRESTED BASILISK *Basiliscus plumifrons*

REP-TILE   Cold-blooded vertebrate that breathes air and usually has a skin covering of scales or bony plates.

AM-PHIB-I-AN   Cold-blooded vertebrate with smooth, scaleless skin, that starts out life in the water as a gill-breathing tadpole. Later, it usually develops lungs and limbs, and spends part of its time on land.

Reptiles (4 orders)	Amphibians (3 orders)
Turtles	Frogs and toads
Crocodilians	Salamanders and newts
Snakes and lizards	Caecilians (worm-like
Tuatura	creatures)

The study of reptiles and amphibians is called **herpetology**, from the Greek word *herpo*, which means to creep or crawl.

RHINOCEROS VIPER   *Bitis nasicornis*

WHAT DOES IT MEAN TO BE COLD-BLOODED?

Scientists call reptiles and amphibians "**ecto-therms**," *ecto* meaning "out" and *therma* meaning "heat"—without heat or *cold-blooded*. But what does that mean?

Most mammals have higher body temperatures than reptiles. To maintain that high body temperature, mammals use half (or more) of the food that they eat to generate body heat. They are warm-blooded (**endotherms**).

Reptiles don't waste food-energy on producing heat. They absorb heat and cold directly from their surroundings. This doesn't mean that they are at the complete mercy of the elements. Reptiles use what scientists call **behavioral temperature control**—seeking out or avoiding sunlight as needed. After a cool night, snakes and lizards bask in the sun to restore a high enough temperature to go on with the business of living—that is, eating and mating.

Because they have gotten around the heat problem, cold-blooded creatures need much less food to survive. This explains why reptiles live so successfully in food-scarce areas—like the desert! If conditions get really bad, amphibians and reptiles can just "shut down," hibernating until the problem of no food or cold weather simply passes.

Of course, even though reptiles can be found almost everywhere—except in the polar regions—the majority live in tropical and semi-tropical parts of the world.

But, strangely enough, while cold may be a problem for reptiles, heat is worse! Although most lizards can withstand body temperatures up to 107°F (42°C), anything higher could be fatal. Desert dwellers are careful to be active only in cooler periods of the day. At noon they find protection in the shade or by burrowing down into cooler sand. Some reptiles avoid the problem altogether by hunting at night!

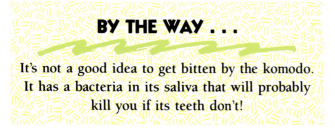

Manfred Gottschalk, TOM STACK AND ASSOCIATES

KOMODO DRAGON *Varanus komodoensis*

A DRAGON LIVES!

The KOMODO DRAGON lives—you guessed it!—on Komodo, an island near Indonesia. It's a tough place to get to and the komodo's last protected habitat.

BY THE WAY . . .

It's not a good idea to get bitten by the komodo. It has a bacteria in its saliva that will probably kill you if its teeth don't!

This huge monitor lizard has a nasty disposition and the size to back it up! In fact, with the full-grown length of a luxury car (12 feet/3.7m) and a weight of 380 pounds (136kg), it is the largest living lizard! It's easy to see how these dragons can, and do, snack on young goats, deer or even people foolish enough to get too close!

That's how the Sultan of the neighboring island of Sumbawa kept his subjects in line. Criminals and other "undesirables" were deported to the uninhabited Komodo, where the ferocious creature, with its keen tracking skills and knife-like claws, would hunt down its unlucky prey.

THE DEVIL'S FROG

What would you do if a fat 10-inch (25.4cm) long frog suddenly jumped out at you! What if it looked like a green devil with horns sticking out of the top of its head, right above the eyes? Well, what you'd better do is jump back! You've just been hopped by the South American AMAZONIAN HORNED FROG, a beautifully colored creature with a very mean streak! It's big on biting fingers and hangs on more like a bulldog than a bullfrog. This fearsome character thinks nothing of eating its brother, which in an odd way is good. At least, this gruesome activity controls the frog's numbers.

ONCE UPON A TIME . . .

The Argentinians, famous for raising beautiful horses, have claimed (wrongly) that the bite of a horned frog, on the lip of a grazing horse, would kill it (the horse, of course!).

AMAZONIAN HORNED FROG   *Ceratophrys cornutas*

D. Barker, TOM STACK AND ASSOCIATES

GIANT LAND TORTOISE *Geochelone elephantopus*

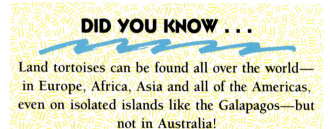

DID YOU KNOW . . .

Land tortoises can be found all over the world—
in Europe, Africa, Asia and all of the Americas,
even on isolated islands like the Galapagos—but
not in Australia!

THE UNDISPUTED CHAMPION

TORTOISES have always been thought to be slow, but they're really not that poky. Some of them can crank up to two miles (3.2km) per hour. That's nearly as fast as you can walk. Not bad, considering that it's lugging a huge shell on its back! The tortoise's specialty is its shell, and that tough armor, modified by nature to suit every environment, has ensured its survival for 175 million years. The bulky shell doesn't come off—it's part of the living animal. The top plate (called the *carapace*) is firmly attached to the backbone and the belly is covered with a piece called the *plastron*. They are joined together at the side by a bony bridge.

BESIDES THAT . . .

The largest land tortoise in the world—51 inches (130cm) shell length—is the Aldabra. It lives in the Seychelles, a group of islands in the Indian Ocean.

Tortoises are also extraordinary because they live longer than any other animal. Reports of 150 years are common! Imagine the famous giant "Tonga Tortoise" that was presented to the ruler of Tonga by the explorer Captain James Cook in 1774. The tortoise was already quite old, but it went on to live through the Revolutionary War, the Civil War, World Wars I and II, the Korean War and Vietnam, not to mention the invention of just about everything we take for granted. This aged tortoise was blind in one eye, had survived two brush fires, being trampled by a horse and run over by a cart! It's believed to be well over 200, but its age can't be confirmed, because all the records on Tonga are oral, not written!

HARD TO BELIEVE, BUT . . .

Tortoises are in danger from hyenas. They can bite completely through the tough shell!

CHUCKWALLA   *Sauromalus obesus*

TAIL OF A LIZARD

Poor lizards! Snakes, birds, mammals, and even bigger lizards—just about everyone preys on them! The lizard called the CHUCKWALLA has an unusual means of dealing with persecution! It doesn't just run away. When it is pursued, it squeezes into the nearest rock crevice, wedging itself in by blowing its body up to half again its normal size. Its scales catch on the rock, making it almost impossible for the hungry enemy to pull it out. If worse comes to worst, as a last resort the chuckwalla does that old lizard favorite—losing its tail—in hopes of being left alone. How does it do that? There's a weak spot in every lizard's tail, sort of like a perforation, where the muscles and blood vessels can come apart neatly and there is very little bleeding at the separation. Obviously, if someone grabs a lizard's tail, it will come off easily at that spot, but lizards have another strategy: If they're taken by the neck, they'll shake their own tail off! When this happens, the tail continues to wiggle and move off in another direction. That often confuses the enemy enough to make it drop the real lizard and go after the tail!

Lizards think twice before dumping their tails. Although the tail grows back and can be dropped off time and time again, it will never get back the original markings, lost vertebrae or specialized tail functions—locomotion, grasping, displaying and social standing too (it may have less opportunity to breed because of its less-than-handsome tail). But, most important of all, many lizard tails store the fat necessary for winter survival, and that can be a tragic loss in a cold climate!

Rod Planck, TOM STACK AND ASSOCIATES

ALLIGATOR SNAPPING TURTLE
Macroclemys temminckii

LURED FOR LUNCH

Whoops! No finger! That's what you'll be saying if you're weird enough to stick your hand in the mouth of the North American ALLIGATOR SNAPPING TURTLE, one of the largest freshwater turtles in the world. This turtle likes a bite of meat and what kind doesn't much matter. Witness the clever way it gets its dinner. The Snapper lies perfectly still down in the mud on the bottom of the pond. It opens its toothless, beak-type mouth and waves a

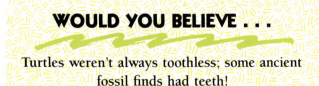

WOULD YOU BELIEVE . . .

Turtles weren't always toothless; some ancient fossil finds had teeth!

small reddish, worm-like stalk, attached to its tongue, as a "lure." Sooner or later, a small fish is sure to come close to investigate what looks to him like a meal. Then, quick as a wink, the turtle has caught its dinner!

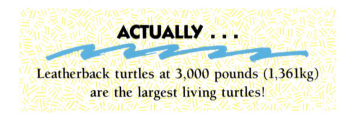

ACTUALLY . . .

Leatherback turtles at 3,000 pounds (1,361kg) are the largest living turtles!

SOLOMON ISLAND SKINK   *Corucia zebrata*

SAND SWIMMERS

What is it? It's spotted, striped, banded or a solid color. It may have legs and it may not. It's a lizard that's called a SKINK! The Solomon Islands' two-foot (.6m) long Giant Skink even has a prehensile tail—a tail like a monkey's that can be used to grasp things. And that is just what it needs for climbing trees and hanging on to branches.

Another skink, the Five-Lined Skink, has a beautiful shiny blue tail when it is young. Its unusual color supposedly attracts predators, but when they grab it, the skink plays an old lizard trick and just lets the tail drop off—it's disposable! This trick that draws the attention to a disposable part is called "deflective coloration"—and it enables the skink to escape from many a dangerous situation.

Skinks are found all over the warmer parts of the world. Some even live in the desert, burying their eggs as deep as six feet (1.8m) underground. They get that deep by wiggling their sleek bodies, "swimming" through the sand.

AS A MATTER OF FACT . . .

Skinks can breathe underground because the loose, dry sand they "swim" in lets some air through.

15

CHARMING SNAKES

Most of us would agree that the COBRA, growing to eight feet (2.4m) or so, is one impressive snake! How brave, or foolhardy, is the snake charmer, swaying rhythmically back and forth with his flute, mesmerizing the snake with the lilting music—*hold it!* Snakes are deaf! That's right, scientists say they have no eardrums, and therefore they can't hear airborne vibrations. If that's so, what is fascinating the snake? The clever snake-charmer keeps his pets inside a dark basket. When the lid is suddenly lifted, the surprised and half-blinded snake rears up in its typical hood-spread, defensive position and fixes on the first moving object it sees—the flute. The snake is not moving with the beat of the music; it's following the motion of the object!

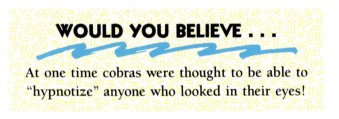

WOULD YOU BELIEVE . . .

At one time cobras were thought to be able to "hypnotize" anyone who looked in their eyes!

Spitting cobras have developed the habit of shooting venom at people or animals that they feel threatened by. Accurate up to 9 feet (2.7m)—they're aiming for the victim's eyes, where the poison is sure to cause pain and temporary (sometimes permanent) blindness. Victims must be tied up to keep from scratching their eyes, which would allow the poison to enter their bloodstream, causing pa-

COBRA   *Naja naja*

SURPRISINGLY . . .

Very few elephants die from snake bite, but some do—from cobras!

MONGOOSE *Helogale parvula*

ralysis and death from suffocation. Staring into the eyes of a cobra is certainly intimidating. Rudyard Kipling tells the story of how the mongoose Rikki-Tikki-Tavi confronts and saves its human family from a pair of cobras. The mongoose avoids the snake's "hypnotic" stare and triumphs by employing bravery, wit and a common mongoose trait—endurance! By quickly jumping back and forth the mongoose keeps the snake on constant alert. The venomous viper finally becomes so tired that it's no longer able to hold its head up in striking position. Then the mongoose jumps the cobra!

AS A MATTER OF FACT . . .

The King Cobra is the largest venomous snake in the world at 16 feet (5m), with a head as large as a man's hand—and it's also the most intelligent!

BULLFROG *Rana catesbeiana*

WHEN IS A FROG NOT A FROG?

Frogs do two things extremely well. They catch insects and avoid birds! That's why they've been around for many millions of years! Of all the animal groups in the world, frogs are the least harmful to humans. Too bad we can't say the same!

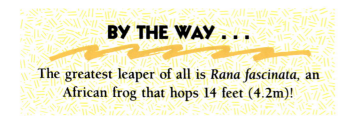

BY THE WAY . . .

The greatest leaper of all is *Rana fascinata,* an African frog that hops 14 feet (4.2m)!

Many animals are born little (and not so little) duplicates of their parents. Amphibians are an exception, and the BULLFROG is a good example. When its 25,000 half-inch eggs float on the surface of the water, encased in their cocoon of jelly, and start to hatch, what comes out are **larvae** that don't look anything like frogs! The frogs' children look like fish! They have flattened tails for swimming, eyes on the sides of their heads and they even breathe through gills!

It could take days, months or even years before the amphibian larva starts to look like its parents. The process is called **metamorphosis**, and the cooler the weather, the longer it takes. In northern climates it takes bullfrog **tadpoles** two years to look like froglets! Here's what happens: First the tail shrinks, as the food stored there is used up by the growing larvae. Then the back legs with their tiny webbed feet pop out on either side of the retracting tail. Soon the right front and finally the left front legs appear. The eyes move from the sides of the head to their prominent, bulging spot on the top. The gills shrink and lungs grow, and the digestive system changes in preparation for the adult's **carnivorous** lifestyle. Tadpoles prefer plants, but the eight-inch-long adult bullfrogs have enormous appetites and eat just about anything that moves, including insects, worms, crayfish, small terrapins and alligators, garter and coral snakes and, believe it or not, an occasional mouse or bird! Before you know it, one of nature's most amazing transformations has taken place and a tiny tadpole has become a full-grown frog!

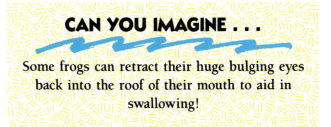

CAN YOU IMAGINE . . .

Some frogs can retract their huge bulging eyes back into the roof of their mouth to aid in swallowing!

BROWN ANOLE *Anolis sagrei*

Joe McDonald, TOM STACK AND ASSOCIATES

YOUR EMOTIONS ARE SHOWING

Like the Old World chameleons, ANOLES use camouflage to hide, changing from green to brown and shades in between, depending upon whether they're sitting on a leaf or tree bark. Anoles also turn brown when the weather is cool (under 70°F/17°C) and bright green on warm sunny days. Surprisingly, the lizard's mood plays a part, too. The loser of an anole argument shows negative emotion by turning brown; the winner remains green, an "up" color!

How does this happen? The **hormone** "intermedin" is responsible. It is produced in the pituitary gland, near the part of the anole's brain that controls emotion. The bloodstream races the hormone to special color cells, causing changes in the pigment.

INTERESTING . . .

The anole has many devices for attracting a mate. One of them is displaying an otherwise hidden, brightly colored flap of skin called a "dewlap." You can see it in this picture.

PRIMITIVE BIOLOGICAL WARFARE

The French explorers of the Caribbean island of Martinique were met by a most inhospitable host. They named it FER DE LANCE, because of its lance-shaped head and body. Perhaps you've guessed that I'm talking about a snake, a **pit viper**, one very poisonous slitherer! The fer de lance is a classic "ambush" predator, sometimes hiding by a mammal trail for weeks until an unfortunate meal happens by! Like all pit vipers, the fer de lance has small depressions, or "pits," on its face between the eye and the nostril. The many nerve endings in the facial pits are so sensitive to the tiniest changes in temperature that they can detect the heat left from a warm-blooded animal that passed over the ground 20 minutes before! If the snake chooses to pursue dinner, a "scent trail" may be picked up by its perceptive tongue!

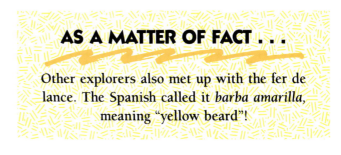

AS A MATTER OF FACT . . .

Other explorers also met up with the fer de lance. The Spanish called it *barba amarilla,* meaning "yellow beard"!

FER DE LANCE   *Bothrops atrox*

TUATARA *Sphenodon punctatus*

THE THIRD EYE

The very last holdout of an ancient group of reptiles that are even older than the dinosaurs, the TUATARA has survived for over 200 million years, with only minor changes in its skeleton, while all the rest of its order Rhynchocephalia have died off. The so-called "beakheaded" reptiles live today in a nature preserve on Stephen's Island and on other small islands off the coast of New Zealand.

At first glance, the tuatara looks just like an ordinary two-foot (.61cm) long lizard, but no—it clearly is not. At least, not to scientists. Tuataras have no external ears as lizards do, and if you cut one open you could see hook-like extensions on its ribs—a bird-like feature. In the top-center of its head is a third eye, covered by a thin layer of skin. All the parts are there, the retina, lens, nerve endings, everything except the muscles. The eye is not used for seeing, and scientists now believe it may be used as a homing device, allowing the animal to judge where it is in relation to the sun.

Tuataras are remarkable for their very low rate of **metabolism**. Normally, they take one breath every seven seconds but, if need be, they can go for an hour without breathing! The islands they live on are not tropical, and tuataras are still active at 52°F (11°C), the lowest recorded temperature for any reptile activity! No wonder they flourished during the Age of Reptiles!

Tuataras are also one of the longest-lived animals. A full-grown two-pound (.9kg) male may be over 100 years old! They won't mate until they're over 20 years old, and even then the eggs won't be laid for a year after fertilization and they take another 15 months to hatch—much, much longer than any other reptile's.

John Cancalosi, TOM STACK AND ASSOCIATES

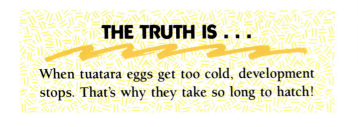

THE TRUTH IS . . .

When tuatara eggs get too cold, development stops. That's why they take so long to hatch!

Tuataras regularly share nesting burrows with sea birds, digging petrels or shearwaters, but there's no problem with overcrowding! The bird goes off fishing during the day and the tuatara goes out feeding at night. When the tuatara hibernates, the bird migrates. It's a perfect arrangement, except that the tuatara has been known to dine on bird eggs!

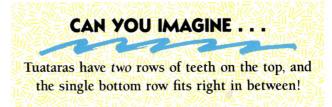

CAN YOU IMAGINE . . .

Tuataras have *two* rows of teeth on the top, and the single bottom row fits right in between!

BANDED SEA SNAKE *Hydrophis cyanocinctus*

SERPENT STOMACH PROBLEMS

For any fish—including sharks—foolish enough to chow-down on the BANDED SEA SNAKE, the results can be disastrous. It's not what you think. Big fish don't have to worry about the venomous sea snake from the *outside* because it can't bite through the tough fish scales. But many fish swallow their dinner in one piece, so the whole snake gets swallowed into the unwary diner's stomach and the irritated snake takes a nip! The snake's deadly venom rushes into the fish's bloodstream, and that's the end of the fish. But it might not be the end of the sea snake! The dying victim may vomit it up and the snake could get the last laugh, as it swims away!

NEVER TRUST A SNAKE

Most SEA SNAKES hang out in relatively shallow water feeding on the fish and their eggs that gather around coral reefs. But some adventurous sea snakes spend their days floating across the open ocean, going wherever the wind or current takes them! It looks as if these snakes are "sitting ducks," but they're not. Many have vividly colored skin to warn predators that they are quite poisonous!

DID YOU KNOW . . .

In some sea snakes, the lung runs almost the entire length of the snake!

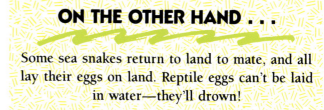

ON THE OTHER HAND . . .

Some sea snakes return to land to mate, and all lay their eggs on land. Reptile eggs can't be laid in water—they'll drown!

Floating sea snakes don't have to search for food. They have their own larder cruising right along with them. You see, small fish tend to gather under any floating object—dead or alive—and soon "adopt" the snake, swimming around its tail (they're too smart to get near its head!). When the snake wants a meal, it begins to swim *backwards*, tricking the fish into thinking that its head is its tail! **ZAP!** Dinner is served!

INDONESIAN SEA SNAKE   *Naen manado*

SIDEWINDER *Crotalus cerastes*

SNAKY MOVES

Lizards developed before snakes, and so did lizard-locomotion! To move ahead, the lizard puts its right front leg forward and its back left foot forward, then vice versa. The result of this action is a wiggle—the forerunner of legless motion. In fact, lizards and snakes are so closely related that they are in the same group—*Squamata*. Some lizards have even lost their legs (worm lizards), while some snakes (like an anaconda) have the remains of lost limbs! Snakes have gone on to perfect living without legs, and have developed four ways of getting around:

Rectilinear locomotion: This is simply moving straight ahead by "walking" on its skin. The broad, flat belly scales on parts of its body slide forward, catching the ground like tractor treads and pulling the rest of the body along (the snake has to have loose skin for this to work). Often used on smooth surfaces, this subtle movement allows heavy snakes, like boas and vipers, to sneak up on prey.

Lateral undulation: This is the familiar snaky motion. The snake uses the irregular surface of the ground to help it move, getting a hold on rocks, twigs, whatever, and pushing against them.

Concertina locomotion: The snake's head stretches outward, uncoiling the tight double-S shape of its body. It gets a "neck hold" and pulls the rest of its body forward into a coiled shape again.

Sidewinding: This interesting movement is great for skimming across the desert's soft sand. There's even a snake named for it—the SIDEWINDER. The snake's S-coiled body turns sideways to go forward. Only two parts of the sidewinder's body touch the hot sand at any one time, leaving behind very distinctive diagonal-ladder marks in the sand.

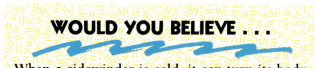

WOULD YOU BELIEVE . . .

When a sidewinder is cold, it can turn its body a darker hue so it absorbs more heat!

DART POISON FROG   *Dendrobates azureus*

A DEATH-DEALING FROG

Imagine a poison so powerful that a drop will kill a person! Called batrachotoxin by scientists, this lethal liquid is produced by the tiny, one-inch (2.5cm) long, KOKOI FROG of Colombia, South America. Dart Poison Frog (its common name) doesn't bite; it doesn't have to. Its poison comes through the pores in its skin. One beautifully colored jumper supplied the native Indians of western Colombia with enough toxin to prepare 50 blow-gun darts by rubbing the tip over the back of the living frog! The big question is, who gets to catch the frogs, especially since even holding one in your hand could be enough to do you in!

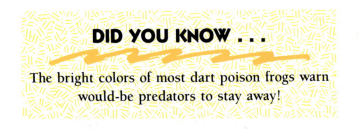

DID YOU KNOW . . .

The bright colors of most dart poison frogs warn would-be predators to stay away!

GROWING UP IN A FLOWER

You can see why one of the most fabulously colored of the dart-poison frogs is named STRAWBERRY DART FROG.

This rain-forest frog takes care of her babies in her own way. She doesn't use the frogs' usual watery pond to incubate them—instead, she lays them on the damp leaf-litter of the forest floor. Now and then she comes by to urinate on them to keep them moist! The hatching larvae have the usual fish-like tadpole shape, but nowhere to swim! What now?

The female Strawberry Dart encourages one tadpole to wriggle onto her back where her sticky mucus-covered skin keeps it in place. As quick and agile as can be, she hop-climbs high into the forest trees looking for an **epiphytic** plant, such as a **bromeliad**. Epiphytes are plants that attach themselves to trees or other plants for support, but get their food and water from the air. Their thick, waxy leaves form a cup that collects rainwater. Into that "baby-bath" steps the mother frog. When the mucus holding the piggybacker in place dissolves, the tiny tadpole is safely swimming in its own nursery pool! Each tadpole is carried to its own plant and left, along with an unfertilized egg for food. The mother delivers more food every few days and before you know it, the young frogs hop down to the forest floor to begin their adult bug-eating days!

STRAWBERRY DART FROG   *Dendrobates pumilio*

GHARIAL   *Gavialis gangeticus*

THE RULING REPTILES

Just by looking, you can see that CROCODILIANS are a living bridge back to the Age of Dinosaurs. In fact, crocs and dinosaurs were both members of the same group of reptiles, the "archosaurs," or "ruling reptiles." The name certainly fits: Crocodilians are the largest, smartest and most advanced of all their kin. Once there were 108 species of crocodilians. Now there are only 23, in three families:

Alligatoridae = alligators and caimans
Crocodylidae = crocodiles
Gavialidae = gharials

The easiest way to tell the three groups apart is to look at their heads. Alligators have wide, flat heads. Their noses are rounded and from the side all you

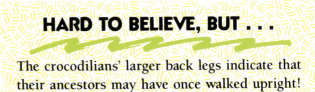

HARD TO BELIEVE, BUT . . .

The crocodilians' larger back legs indicate that their ancestors may have once walked upright!

can see are the upper teeth—the lower ones fit inside the mouth.

The triangular, pointy snout belongs to the crocodile; you can see its teeth, top and bottom, on the outside.

No one could mistake the gharial's oddly shaped nose. It's very long and thin with a bulb on the end, and its hundred pointy teeth are all the same size.

EL LAGARTO—THE LIZARD

El lagarto is what the exploring Spaniards called the thousands of ALLIGATORS decorating the river banks of the New World. Alligators are one of only a few crocodilians that live well outside the tropics. There are two species: One, the Chinese Alligator, is only found in the lower Yangtze River valley of eastern China and is very rare. The other lives in the southern part of the United States.

Amazingly, the sex of alligator babies is determined by the temperature in the nest. This is called **TSD (temperature-dependent sex determination)**. Eggs incubated at 90–93°F (32–34°C) are males, and those kept at temperatures of 82–86°F (28–30°C) are females; 87–89°F (30.5–31.6°C) produces equal numbers of males and females. The sun hitting the top of the nest makes it the hottest—boys; the bottom is coolest—girls!

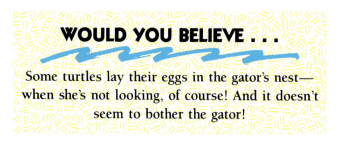

WOULD YOU BELIEVE . . .

Some turtles lay their eggs in the gator's nest—when she's not looking, of course! And it doesn't seem to bother the gator!

AMERICAN ALLIGATOR   *Alligator mississippiensis*

CROCS ON THE NILE

The Greeks first met up with CROCODILES while travelling in Egypt 2,000 years ago. The huge Nile River crocs reminded them of the tiny wall lizards in their homeland called "Krocodeilos." And that's how it happened that one of the largest living reptiles got its name from one of the smallest.

Many crocodiles dig their nests in the sand, and, like the alligator, the heat in the nest determines the sex of the babies. But in this case, the hottest eggs produce girls. Could TDS (temperature-dependent sex determination) partially explain the amazingly quick and total disappearance of the dinosaurs 65 million years ago? What if TDS applied to dinosaur eggs too? Then the cooling (or heating) of the earth, whatever caused it—a meteor, a natural disaster or climate changes—could have produced all boys or all girls. And that would have been that!

NILE CROCODILE   *Crocodylus niloticus*

Joe McDonald. TOM STACK AND ASSOCIATES

Kerry T. Givens, TOM STACK AND ASSOCIATES

THORNY DEVIL *Molloch horridus*

LEGENDARY LIZARDS

This incredibly spiked and spiny Australian lizard was named after an ancient god of child sacrifice. The name is quite inappropriate though, because the *Molloch horridus* is only eight inches (20cm) long and eats only ants—1,500 per meal!

The thorny protuberances all over the lizard's body aren't there just for defense: They're arranged in such a way that dew or rain is gradually channelled down the valleys until it gets to the THORNY DEVIL's mouth. Nice feature for a desert dweller!

BY THE WAY . . .

Lizards have long tails—snakes, short ones!

SALAMANDER   *Eurycea bilineata*

HOW HOT IS HOT?

The word SALAMANDER is a general name for an entire group of creatures that includes newts and sirens (pages 35 and 45). These amphibians look like moist lizards with long tails but no scales or claws. Their legs are so short that their bellies drag on the ground. Salamanders can grow back almost any body part—arms, legs, tails, even eye retinas and severed optic nerves. Some people call them "spring lizards," because they are often seen around natural springs.

Even today some people believe that the bite of the bright-colored salamander is the "kiss of death"! Here's some news for you: Salamanders have quite small teeth and don't bite hard, don't sting and don't have fangs. But they do have a fiery liquid called salamindrin that comes out of the pores located behind their ears. It's not a good idea to get this burning, nasty stuff in your eyes or mouth or in a cut, but if you're smart enough not to stick a salamandered finger up your nose, no harm will come from picking up the lizard lookalike.

NEWTS TO YOU

The newt looks a lot like the salamander but its life is more complicated. Instead of having the usual amphibian two-stage life cycle, it has three stages!

As the newly hatched larva of the RED-SPOTTED NEWT grows, it soon transforms into a creature called an eft. The lizard-shaped eft leaves its watery home for a life on the land. Warning, warning! The eft's beautiful red skin—unusually rough and dry for an amphibian—is poisonous! Most animals are smart enough to steer clear of it. The eft's only real worry is skunks, which simply tear the eft apart and, skipping the poison skin, eat only the insides. Eventually, after several years, the eft's skin changes again to a smooth, slick, greenish brown, non-toxic covering. The tail grows broad and flat for swimming and the red-spotted newt returns to the larval pond of its youth to live out its remaining days!

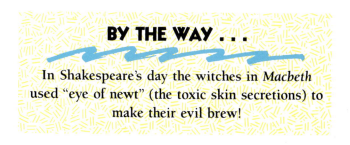

BY THE WAY . . .

In Shakespeare's day the witches in *Macbeth* used "eye of newt" (the toxic skin secretions) to make their evil brew!

RED-SPOTTED NEWT   *Notophthalmus viridescens*

CANE TOAD *Bufo marinus*

LOADS OF TOADS

It's a really big deal for any country to lose one of its principal crops, and that's exactly what was happening to the sugar crop in Australia in 1935. The hungry cane beetle was eating every bit of sugarcane it could get, so the growers brought in 100 CANE TOADS from Hawaii, in hopes that they would live up to their reputation and eat the cane beetles before any more damage was done. No such luck! The eight-inch (20.3cm) toads ignored the

DID YOU KNOW . . .

Most toads secrete a milky toxin from a gland behind their eyes. If any creatures take a bite of them, they have to spit out the burning mouthful!

beetles and concentrated on snakes and frogs. Now the toads are everywhere, busily laying 54,000 eggs at a time. If anything or anyone tries to eat them, they promptly secrete a poison potent enough to kill a dog in 15 minutes. Now there's a real mess—as often happens when people try to fool with Mother Nature, the problem is compounded!

SURPRISINGLY ENOUGH . . .

Toads eat their own shed skin for the valuable nutrients contained in it!

CAN YOU IMAGINE . . .

When confronted by a hungry snake, clever toads gulp air into their stomach and intestines, blowing themselves up too big to be swallowed!

Chip Isenhart, TOM STACK AND ASSOCIATES

BY THE WAY . . .

Of the mother toad's thousands of eggs, only 10 may make it to adulthood!

LOGGERHEAD   *Caretta caretta*

IT'S THE OCEAN LIFE FOR ME

The big sea turtles spend most of their lives in the ocean, where their heavy, 300- to 1,500-pound (136–681kg) shapes become amazingly graceful supported by the water. Some of the turtles are called LOGGERHEADS. They nest on beaches around the world. In the United States from April to August, the nomads come close to the shore on both coasts to feed around the reefs and rocks guarding the nesting beaches. Swimming mostly with their front flippers, the turtles can home in on the short section of any nesting beach that they prefer.

The female doesn't have to rush, since she has the ability to lay her eggs up to six years after fertilization! But once she is ready to do it, she waits until dark to start the slow trek onto the sand, lugging her huge body 300 feet (92m) up the beach past the high-tide line.

If you should ever be lucky enough to see this event, don't even think of petting the large lady. For one thing, you'd probably scare her back into the water and no eggs would be laid (worse for her). Or (worse for you) she'd live up to her name in Sri Lanka—"Dog Turtle"—and bite your finger off!

Once she's made it to the nesting site, she's got to finish her task and get back in the water before dawn when birds, dogs and beachcombers will come along and find the secret nest. Thirty minutes are spent shovelling out a six-inch (15cm) deep hole as big as her body. Then the hind flippers dig down eight more inches (20cm) to form the egg pit. Legend says that she'll be "crying," because of her offsprings' risky future. In reality, the thick fluid oozing from her eyes keeps them clean and rids her kidneys of excess salt. The eggs themselves fall down into the prepared hole. They're tough, not brittle like hens eggs, but rubbery and flexible. Thirty more minutes to lay the 120 eggs and the concealment begins. She has to fill the egg-pit and then the body hole with sand. Finally, she must disturb and scatter the surrounding sand in every direction, to hide any traces.

BY THE WAY . . .

When the baby turtles hatch 8–10 weeks later, they make a midnight dash for their home in the ocean. The males will most likely *never* set foot on land again!

At last the mother turtle returns to the sea. She will probably come back on land again three to ten times this breeding season and lay up to 800 eggs. Then, exhausted from the effort, she'll take several years off.

THE ART OF BEING INVISIBLE

Many snakes, especially the "ambush" vipers, rely on the camouflage-coloration of their skin to avoid being seen. There's no way, for instance, to spot a COPPERHEAD lying motionless in a pile of autumn leaves!

The snake's outer skin is made of **keratin**, a substance like fingernails, which has thickened and formed scales. Unlike our skin, the snake's doesn't grow along with its body, so the snake has to change its skin—sometimes four times a year—to keep up with its own growth. The process, called **molting**,

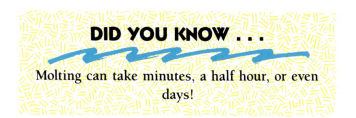

DID YOU KNOW . . .

Molting can take minutes, a half hour, or even days!

actually starts days before the main event takes place. The copperhead's body starts to look dull and lifeless and its eyes get cloudy. It becomes irritable and loses its appetite. Finally, the big day arrives! The copperhead rubs its mouth on a rough surface until the skin comes loose. Slowly, like turning a sock inside out, it wriggles out of its skin. The new skin is much brighter and, of course, looser—to accommodate future new growth. What's left behind is a complete piece of inside-out old skin, right down to and including the eye coverings!

Joe/Carol McDonald, TOM STACK AND ASSOCIATES

COPPERHEAD   *Agkistrodon contortrix*

AMAZING AS IT SOUNDS . . .

A completely severed snake head can still bite a half hour later!

GILA MONSTER   *Heloderma suspectum*

POISONOUS PETS

Only two out of more than 3,000 lizards are poisonous! The GILA MONSTER, living in the arid regions of Mexico and the southwestern United States, is one of them. Now, why would anyone want a poisonous lizard for a pet, especially considering some of the awful stories that have been told about it. For example:

- The gila monster is a cross between a lizard and a crocodile. (It's not.)
- It's poisonous because it can't get rid of body waste. (No, it's poisonous, all right, but this is the wrong reason.)
- It has really bad breath, for the same reason. (Still wrong!)
- It leaps on its victim, spits venom from its poisonous tongue and is quite impossible to kill! (All untrue.)

Sound like good enough reasons *not* to keep a gila monster around the house? Nevertheless, by 1952 so many gila monsters had been sold as pets that they were close to extinction and placed on the endangered list!

GREEN TREE PYTHON   *Chondropython viridus*

TAKING MATTERS INTO HER OWN COILS

By basking in the sun or sheltering in the shade, most reptiles are able to achieve a body temperature of as much as 30°F warmer—or cooler—than the surrounding air. The GREEN TREE PYTHON is one of an amazing group of snakes (including the Indian and Blood pythons) that are able to produce heat on their own! This very special trait is used for only one purpose: to care for the creature's eggs. This ability allows the python to live in a cooler climate than some other egg-laying snakes.

After she lays her eggs, the female python wraps her coils around the **clutch** and stays put for months, instead of slithering off like most snakes do. By intense shivering, she is able to raise her body temperature up to 13°F (7°C)—high enough to keep the eggs at the heat they need to develop. Unfortunately, their mother will lose half her body weight from the effort, and it will take her three to five years to recover enough to try it again.

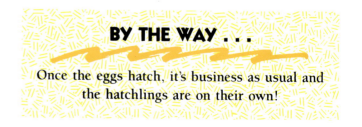

BY THE WAY . . .

Once the eggs hatch, it's business as usual and the hatchlings are on their own!

GOING HOME

By some miracle of nature, GREEN SEA TURTLES, which feed off the eastern coast of South America, navigate across the Atlantic Ocean to Ascension Island, three-quarters of the way and 1400 miles towards Africa, for nesting! How do they do it? Scientists believe that they may have several means of finding their way: Along the coast they simply follow the shoreline. In the open ocean they may use the sun as a compass, or possibly, landmarks on the ocean floor. Magnetically sensitive particles in their brains could be responding to the earth's magnetic field. Or, is it possible they are "smelling" the ocean currents and the odor of far-off lands?

GREEN SEA TURTLE *Chelonia mydas*

Joe McDonald, TOM STACK AND ASSOCIATES

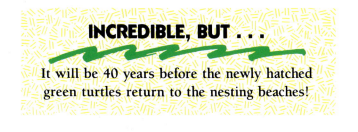

INCREDIBLE, BUT . . .

It will be 40 years before the newly hatched green turtles return to the nesting beaches!

Celestial navigation is not likely, because turtle eyesight is adapted for underwater vision and they are quite nearsighted out of water. You can see that if turtles are indeed "sniffing" their way home, ocean **pollution** could be disastrous for this already endangered species!

Dave B. Fleetham, TOM STACK AND ASSOCIATES

FROGS AND TOADS

Frogs are kind of cute, but nobody seems very fond of the warty TOAD. You know the difference, don't you? Frogs have smooth, moist skin, long, specialized legs for leaping and toe pads for climbing. Toads, on the other hand, seem to have drier, bumpy skin; they're more short-legged and heavy-set, with a prominent, rounded poison-producing gland located below the ears.

There are about 3,800 species of hoppers and they live everywhere except for the polar regions, Greenland and some oceanic islands. The GOLDEN TOAD is found only in the Monteverde Cloud Forest in Costa Rica, where it is never seen except for the few days each year that it comes out to find a mate. Its last appearance was in 1987—no one's seen it since! Where is it hiding? Is it extinct? This is another of nature's mysteries.

AMERICAN TOAD   *Bufo americanus*

GOLDEN TOAD   *Bufo periglenes*

THE UGLIEST SIREN YOU EVER SAW

The sirens of Greek mythology were beautiful, sweet-singing water nymphs. These SIRENS, on the other hand, look like eels with stubby front legs. They don't say much—just croak a bit—and, like "Peter Pan," they never grow up, staying for all their lives in the infantile larval form. These eternally juvenile amphibians live in the southeastern United States in shallow rivers and ditches, eating worms, snails and algae.

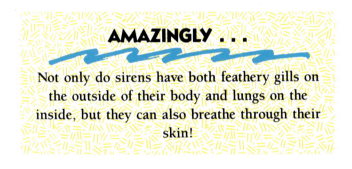

AMAZINGLY . . .

Not only do sirens have both feathery gills on the outside of their body and lungs on the inside, but they can also breathe through their skin!

Sirens are always coated with a slippery, slimy soap-like mucus that makes them almost impossible to hold on to. If the rains don't come and the old watering hole dries up, sirens survive by digging down a foot (.3m) or so in the mud and going to sleep for a couple of months. Their mucus coating turns into a hard covering that protects them by completely sealing in their remaining body moisture!

David M. Dennis, TOM STACK AND ASSOCIATES

DWARF SIREN   *Pseudobrachus striatus*

FASTER THAN A SPEEDING BULLET

To a bug a "safe" distance away, the CHAMELEON looks harmless enough. In fact, the potential snack probably doesn't even *see* the camouflaged chameleon until the lizard's tongue shoots out of its mouth faster than your eye can follow. How does it do that? The tongue is hollow, like a straw. It bunches up in the chameleon's mouth the way an accordion closes, and it fires with the speed of a bullet—in only 1/100th of a second! The tongue is actually longer than the lizard! At the end of it is a sticky bulb of glue-like stuff that is capable of holding on to a meal of insects and sometimes a small animal.

Like the anole, this master of disguise can blend in perfectly with its surroundings, even becoming blotched with color to merge into the background. Specialized cells called "chromatophores" make it possible. Now where did that bug go?

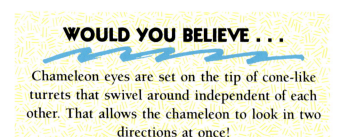

WOULD YOU BELIEVE . . .

Chameleon eyes are set on the tip of cone-like turrets that swivel around independent of each other. That allows the chameleon to look in two directions at once!

JACKSON'S CHAMELEON   *Chameleo jacksoni*

Chip/Jill Isenhart, TOM STACK AND ASSOCIATES

TEXAS HORNED TOAD   *Phrynosoma cornutum*

A THORN IN THE THROAT

Even snakes don't try to eat the TEXAS HORNED TOAD. It's really a lizard that lives in North and Central America from southern Canada to Panama. It's so spiked and spiny that if its spines were to get stuck in the snake's throat, it would be "curtains" for the snake! The toad's favorite food is ants; it loves them and eats them whenever it can. Then spiky

AS A MATTER OF FACT . . .

Horned toads love barren desert habitats; some can withstand temperatures up to 116°F (47°C)!

BY THE WAY . . .

Not only do lizards have an upper eyelid—but most come with a lower one, too! It's transparent to keep out burrs, thorns and dust.

runs back to its underground home. Any animal catching it out in the open is in for a big surprise. The startled horned toad has a scare tactic of its own! It puffs right up, restricting the blood flow out of its head, raising the pressure and bursting the delicate capillaries in its eyes. Out squirts the blood! Look out! Its aim is right on target up to seven feet (2.1m)!

47

GREY-BANDED KING SNAKE *Lampropeltis mexicana*

WHO'S KING OF THE HILL?

There are lots of poisonous snakes out there—
rattlesnakes, coral snakes, mambas, taipans, water
moccasins—but none of them are "top-dog." Why?
Because the KING SNAKE is. It may seem harmless
to us, but it eats poisonous snakes by the bushel!

SURPRISINGLY . . .

Snakes don't have to open their mouths to flick
their tongues. They have a notch in the upper lip
to put it through!

You see, it's immune to their venom. King snakes are constrictors; that means they disable their intended dinner by suffocating it—even other snakes.

The constrictor does not kill by crushing. Instead, every time the victim breathes out, the snake tightens its coils, preventing the ribs from expanding again. Pretty soon there's no room in the victim's chest for air. Goodbye, prey!

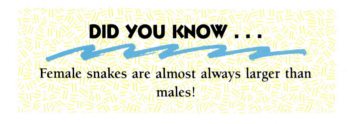

DID YOU KNOW . . .

Female snakes are almost always larger than males!

CAN YOU IMAGINE . . .

Some snakes have 400 vertebrae—humans only have 33!

Occasionally, nature will pull a fast one and a very unusual animal will be born, as in the case of the two-headed snake. It was doing just fine until the day when Head #1 decided that Head #2 would make an easy snack and tried to swallow it. Observers rescued Head #2 only to have it later take revenge on Head #1, with fatal results for both heads and the shared body!

RATSNAKE *Elaphe obsoleta*

EASTERN DIAMONDBACK RATTLESNAKE   *Crotalus adamanteus*

ARMED AND DANGEROUS

Copperheads, water moccasins and rattlers are all venomous snakes. Their poison-delivery teeth are so long that they have to fold back into a sheath of skin in the mouth to keep from sticking *themselves!* A snake's fangs are so important to its survival that it always has a spare growing alongside the old tooth.

RATTLESNAKES are known for their habit of

INTERESTINGLY . . .

One group of rattlers that live on an island in the Gulf of California with no population of large animals have lost their rattles!

shaking the rattles on their tails. This defensive maneuver keeps the snake from getting stepped on and accidentally injured by a large animal—a cow, for instance. The rattles are made of keratin, a substance similar to human fingernails. Each one of the loosely interlocked shells was once a scale that has enlarged and thickened. Every time the snake sheds its skin (molts), a scale is retained and a new rattle is formed. The rattles hit against each other, making the characteristic buzzing sound. Depending on the size of the snake, the rattling can be heard from three to 160 yards (.9–49m) away!

Brian Parker, TOM STACK AND ASSOCIATES

LEGEND HAS IT . . .

Rattlers coil clockwise in the Northern Hemisphere and counterclockwise in the Southern!

By the way, don't bother to try to guess how old a snake is from the number of rattles. Some snakes shed as many as four times a year. Besides, rattles wear out and break off all the time. Usually, a wild snake has no more than 14, though, in its own best interests, eight is perhaps the ideal number for maximum sound and effect.

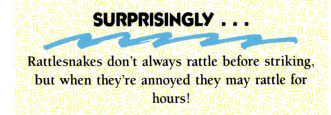

SURPRISINGLY . . .

Rattlesnakes don't always rattle before striking, but when they're annoyed they may rattle for hours!

EGG-EATING SNAKE   *Dasypeltis scabra*

ONE WAY TO EAT AN EGG

Unlike lizards, snakes can't tear their food into bite-sized pieces to eat it. Their only choice is to swallow it whole and they do, amazing human observers with the enormous size of some of their dinners. The African EGG-EATING SNAKE is able to swallow a smooth bird's egg twice as large as itself! Even though we think of eggs as delicate and brittle, their oval shape makes them surprisingly resistant to damage and crushing. The snake's feat is like bobbing for apples without using your hands, but in a way the egg-eating snake has an even bigger problem—it has almost no teeth! So, how does it grab hold of the slippery egg? In place of teeth are thick folds of muscular gum tissue. The folds act like suction cups pulling the egg steadily into the snake's mouth. Now, how to get *inside* the egg! As the egg starts down the snake's throat, sharp projections that stick out of the snake's backbone pierce the shell and the liquid inside flows down into the snake's belly. The remaining, but useless, shell is neatly compressed and regurgitated all in one piece!

WHO'S GOT A HOLE IN THE HEAD?

A GECKO, that's who! One African species has such thin skin and straight ear openings that you can see light coming right through from the other side of its head! From the smallest one-inch (2.54cm) long to the largest 14-inch (35.5cm), geckos can cling to almost any surface. No, they don't have suction-cup feet! But they do have fine ridges and tiny bristles that cover their soles. These bristles fill every nook and cranny of the surface that the gecko is climbing on and hold it in place. To let go, the gecko curls its toes and releases the tension that is keeping it attached. This is a very practical asset when chasing a buggy dinner up the wall!

MADAGASCAR DAY GECKO   *Phelsuma dubia*

MADAGASCAR LEAF GECKO   *Uroplatus fimbriatus*

STRANGELY ENOUGH . . .

Geckos twitch their tails just like cats before lunging at prey!

BELIEVE IT OR NOT . . .

The Tokay Gecko (*Gecko gecko*) named itself by the sound it makes: "Gecko, gecko!"

MARINE IGUANA   *Amblyrhynchus cristatus*

WATER DRAGON

The volcanic Galapagos Islands, west of South America in the Pacific Ocean, straddle the Equator. It's blisteringly hot on the land and bracingly cold in the water, brought up from the Antarctic by the Humboldt Current. Here lives the only lizard completely adapted to life in the sea. The MARINE IGUANA isn't really that good a swimmer, but it is a fabulous diver! It uses its flattened tail to submerge down to 45 feet (13.7m) when it goes after the short reddish limestone-rich algae that it eats.

Each Galapagos island has its own type of marine iguana, isolated by water from the others. There are eight kinds in all, easily recognized by their different colors. The differences have evolved because, even though these iguanas are at home in the water, they will not swim the distance to the other islands! Scientists think the lizards must have floated to the isolated islands on driftwood "boats." When they didn't find normal lizard food (insects and such) on the geologically "new" volcanic islands, they took to the water in search of something to eat!

STRANGELY ENOUGH . . .

When the marine iguana's eggs hatch, there are equal numbers of males and females, but by adulthood there are far more females. Scientists guess it's because the males dive deeper than the females—right down to where the sharks cruise!

These lizards aren't lonely: The friendly, fun-loving sea lions are the iguanas' constant companions. Talk about two different personalities! The sea lion loves to annoy the lizard. The seal's idea of a good time is to poke and prod a sunning iguana until it tries to escape by running for the water. And that's exactly what the sea lion wants! It follows the lizard into the ocean, pulling on its tail and playing "cat and mouse" with it. Don't worry! The dragon is never hurt—only its dignity is wounded!

THE LIZARD IS A LADY

Reptiles, like all animals, have many different ways of protecting themselves. Some, like the chameleon, use color as camouflage, automatically blending in with their surroundings. Some, like the Dart Poison Frog, use their bright colors as a warning, signalling danger to their enemies. Others, like the Komodo Dragon or the rattlesnake, use their size or poison to stand their ground, prepared to fight.

One little Australian lizard that lives in the tropic woodlands has a different defense tactic. Along its neck lie deep folds of extra skin, supported by thin bony ribs. When facing trouble, the FRILLED LIZ-ARD throws its head back, opens it mouth and blasts the huge—almost as large as its whole body—neck ruff open. This surprise display has the same effect as a lady popping open her parasol in the face of an pesky suitor. The result? Stunned shock—giving the lady (or the lizard) time to make a hasty retreat!

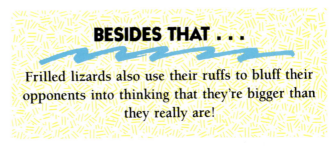

BESIDES THAT . . .

Frilled lizards also use their ruffs to bluff their opponents into thinking that they're bigger than they really are!

FRILLED LIZARD   *Clamydosaurus kingii*

John Cancalosi; TOM STACK AND ASSOCIATES

YELLOW ANACONDA   *Eunectes notaeus*

SUPER SERPENT

This is it—the snake that nightmares are made of! The South American ANACONDA, a member of the boa family, is usually about 18 feet (5.2m) long, but once in a while a snake is found that is double that length!

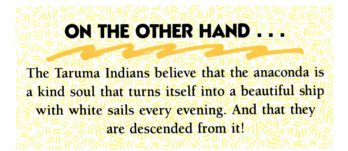

ON THE OTHER HAND . . .

The Taruma Indians believe that the anaconda is a kind soul that turns itself into a beautiful ship with white sails every evening. And that they are descended from it!

An average-size anaconda can kill and eat a full-sized caiman (a South American crocodilian). How can it do that! It's simple for this super serpent. It hunts in two ways. Hanging out around the edge of the sluggish, swampy water it prefers, occasionally dangling from a tree, the snake waits patiently until a rodent, bird, deer, or whatever comes along for a drink. Then ZAP! It grabs the unlucky prey in its mouth and drags it to the bottom of the pond to drown it.

If that doesn't work, anacondas go out looking for food. Whatever it catches gets wrapped in its coils and squeezed until it can't breathe anymore. Then comes the interesting part. Like all snakes, the anaconda swallows its meal whole! Yes, even a deer! By unhinging its jaw, it can open its mouth wide enough for really huge prey to fit in headfirst—even if the victim is larger around than the snake's body *and* even if it's still alive and kicking! Wow, that's an almost unbelievable picture! And the snake handles it all with ease! Not only is its brain encased in bone to protect it, but there's also a valve on the breathing tube that allows it to go right on breathing, despite the large object squeezing down its throat!

A caiman will take a week or more to digest, and a meal that large can last the snake up to a year, if nothing else happens along. Naturally, there are plenty of horror stories about humans disappearing—victims of the "wowlah" (one of the anaconda's local names). Well, there's only been one *documented* case of a human being taken. The proof consisted of strangulation marks on the body, and the snake had not made any attempt to swallow the person. But that doesn't take into account all the *unexplained* mysterious disappearances in anaconda country!

THE FROG THAT PREDICTS THE WEATHER

Spadefoot toads are nicknamed RAIN FROGS even though they don't live anywhere near water. Some even live in desert sand dunes. So how did they get their name? They came to be known as rain frogs because people thought they could actually predict rain! Before a shower hundreds of toads would start calling, burping out their weather forecast, "Rain-today, rain-today." Some African farmers believe rain frogs don't just forecast, but actually *control* the weather. A dry season means especially good care for the hoppers!

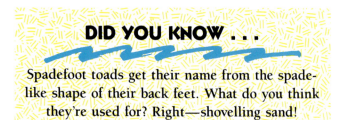

DID YOU KNOW . . .

Spadefoot toads get their name from the spade-like shape of their back feet. What do you think they're used for? Right—shovelling sand!

SPADEFOOT TOAD   *Scaphiopus couchi*

NECESSITY IS THE MOTHER OF INVENTION

Pterosaurs are a group of extinct flying reptiles and that is just what their name means, "flying lizard." The first fossil pterosaur ever found was named PTERODACTYL (it lived 160–65 million years ago). Pterodactyls are classed as reptiles, but scientists believe that they were warm-blooded with a covering of fur! They took to the air on leathery wings stretched between finger bones, featuring claws at the mid-point. The long snout resembled a bird's beak, but was filled with tiny teeth, and the bones were hollow and light enough for the animal to get airborne. To achieve the vision and coordination required to fly, Pterodactyls had to have a much larger brain than other reptiles of the same size.

The photograph here is of a scientific reconstruction based on the fossilized bones of Pterodactylus.

PTERODACTYL   *Pterodactylus*

WOULD YOU BELIEVE . . .

John Cancalosi, TOM STACK AND ASSOCIATES

GLASS SNAKE *Ophisaurus ventralis*

The AUSTRALIAN TREE DRAGON has a tail four times its own length!

At night the ALLIGATOR's eyes glow rosy-pink, a great aid to poachers. The cause is reflected "rhodopsin"—the chemical that makes night vision possible!

When a 120-pound person closes his mouth, the jaw pressure is around 60 pounds, but when a 120-pound CROCO-DILE does the same, the pressure rises slightly—to 1,500 pounds! Imagine getting bitten by that!

GLASS SNAKES are very stiff, because each scale contains a little bone called an "osteo-derm." Thank goodness they have a groove running down the side or they'd be too stiff to move!

AND BESIDES THAT, DID YOU KNOW . . .

GATOR tails can propel the alligator's whole body vertically out of the water!

DWARF PUFF ADDERS (snakes) retreat into the sand tail first!

Most crocs are slow and awkward on land, but JOHNSTON'S CROCODILE (Australia) is capable of a full gallop, like a horse!

ANACONDAS, PYTHONS and BOAS have left-over tiny hind legs. They no longer use them to get around, but they can move them!

A green covering of fuzzy algae disguises the CHINESE SWAMP SNAKE from the small fish it eats!

The fastest snakes alive, BLACK MAMBAS, cruise at 7 miles (11km) per hour, and have a sprint speed of 15 miles (24km) per hour!

Some TREE FROGS shed their skin every evening!

RED-EYED TREE FROG   *Agalychnis callidryas*

AMERICAN CROCODILE   *Crocodylus acutus*

IT'S THE WAY OF THE WORLD

The world that we live in is 4.6 *thousand million* years old, a constantly changing place where extinction is the rule and existence the amazing exception! When the ancestors of early amphibians and reptiles inched their way from the warm ancient seas 365 million years ago they faced an incredible challenge—survival! Evolution is all about survival and that's why creatures change, grow and reproduce.

Here's how it works: Some animals possess a trait that makes it easier to get along. Perhaps they're larger, quicker, have sharper teeth or longer claws, or eat food that no one else wants. They have a much better chance of living than their brothers. Maybe

they can even live long enough to pass the valuable characteristic on to their offspring! The tiniest change may take millions of years, but, with luck, the adaptation finally becomes normal for the species.

Whenever their surroundings change—become hotter, drier, colder—animals must change, too! The early reptiles were so successful at adaptation that they expanded into 16 orders of every size, shape and description. Then the environment changed, and thousands of species of dinosaurs and other animals could not adapt quickly enough to avoid extinction. When the "ruling reptiles" vanished a mere 65 million years ago, the less "significant" mammals found themselves with a whole world to expand into—and they did!

Glossary

autotomy. The breaking off of a damaged or trapped body part: the tail of a lizard, claw of a crab.

behavioral temperature control. Influencing internal body temperature by specific actions.

bromeliad. A plant of the pineapple family.

carnivorous. Flesh-eating.

celestial navigation. Navigation by the apparent position of heavenly bodies.

clutch. A group of eggs incubated at the same time.

dewlap. Hanging fold of skin under the neck of some animals.

epiphytical. Non-parasitic plant that grows above the ground on another plant or structure, obtaining nutrients from the air, rain and dust.

Galapagos. A group of islands west of South America in the Pacific Ocean, straddling the equator.

hibernate. To spend the winter in a dormant condition.

hormone. Any internally secreted compound formed in the endocrine glands that affects specifically receptive organs.

invertebrates. Animals without backbones.

keratin. A tough, insoluble protein that is the main constituent of hair, nails, horn and hoofs.

larvae. The young of an animal that undergoes metamorphosis.

metabolism. The process by which a living being uses food to obtain energy, build tissue and dispose of waste.

metamorphosis. Profound change in form from one stage to the next in the life history of an organism.

molting. To cast or shed the feathers, skin or the like in the process of renewal or growth.

mucus. A sticky, slippery substance. In humans, it is usually produced by membranes in the nose and throat.

pit viper. Any of various vipers that have a heat-sensitive pit above each nostril.

pollution. The introduction of harmful substances into the environment.

prehensile. Adapted for seizing, grasping or taking hold of.

Seychelles. A group of islands and inlets located in the Indian Ocean about 900 miles (1,450km) off the coast of Africa.

tadpoles. Larvae of frogs and toads.

TSD (temperature-dependent sex determination). Offspring's sex determined by outside temperature rather than other factors.

vertebrates. Animals with backbones.

BUSH VIPER *Atheris squamigera*

Index